Conversational Dutch

A Comprehensive Guide to Speaking Dutch Fluently

Willow Gardner

Contents

CHAPTER 1

Introduction to Dutch

The Significance of Dutch in Global Communication, Business, and Culture

Why Learn Dutch

Learning Dutch offers a multitude of benefits that extend beyond just language proficiency. Understanding the importance of Dutch in international business, culture, and communication helps motivate students to work hard at learning the language. Dutch is widely spoken around the world and is important for both travel and employment prospects.

Here's an exploration of why learning Dutch holds such importance:

1. Global Communication:

- **Widespread Usage:** While Dutch is primarily spoken in the Netherlands and Belgium (Flanders region), it's also an official language in Suriname and the Dutch Caribbean islands, making it more prevalent than one might initially realize.

- **International Relations:** The Netherlands is a prominent player in international affairs, with a strong presence in diplomacy, trade, and global organizations like the European Union (EU) and the United Nations (UN). Proficiency in Dutch can facilitate communication in these spheres.

2. Business and Career Opportunities:

- **Thriving Economies:** The Netherlands and Belgium boast vibrant economies with diverse sectors, including technology, finance, agriculture, and healthcare. Fluency in Dutch opens doors to employment opportunities within these industries.

- **Multinational Companies:** Many multinational corporations have headquarters or major operations in Dutch-speaking regions. Knowledge of Dutch can be an asset when seeking employment in these companies.

3. Travel and Cultural Enrichment:

- **Ease of Travel:** The ability to converse in Dutch enhances travel experiences in Dutch-speaking countries, allowing for deeper interactions with locals and a better understanding of their culture.

- **Cultural Immersion:** Learning Dutch opens doors to a rich cultural heritage, including literature, art, music, and traditions. It provides a deeper appreciation of Dutch history and society.

4. Academic and Educational Opportunities:

- **Higher Education:** Dutch universities offer a wide range of courses taught in Dutch. Proficiency in the language can enable access to quality education in these institutions.

- **Research and Scholarly Pursuits:** Some fields of study may have valuable resources and research material available only in Dutch, making language proficiency crucial for academic pursuits.

5. Personal Development and Connections:

- **Building Relationships:** Speaking Dutch allows for stronger connections with Dutch-speaking individuals, fostering personal and professional relationships.

- **Cognitive Benefits:** Learning a new language enhances cognitive abilities such as memory, problem-solving, and multitasking, contributing to overall mental agility.

Dutch is important for international communication, commerce, and culture since it can lead to new options in terms of academic pursuits, job advancement, cultural immersion, and personal development. Speaking and being able to understand Dutch can open up a world of opportunities and improve both personal and professional life.

Overview of the Dutch Language

The Germanic language family includes the Dutch language, which is well-known for its distinctive traits and lengthy history. Gaining knowledge about its linguistic origins and relationships with other languages will help you better understand its evolution and structure.

Linguistic Roots and Historical Context:

- **Germanic Origins:** Dutch belongs to the West Germanic branch of the Germanic languages, which also includes English, German, and Frisian. Its roots trace back to the early Germanic tribes that inhabited the regions of present-day Netherlands, Belgium, and parts of Germany.

- **Influence of Old Frankish and Old Saxon:** Dutch evolved from the Old Frankish dialects spoken in the Low Countries during the early Middle Ages. Additionally, Old Saxon, spoken in regions east of the Netherlands, influenced the development of Dutch.

Relation to Other Languages:

- **Similarities with German and English:** Dutch shares many similarities with both German and English due to their common Germanic heritage. Vocabulary, grammar structures, and phonetic elements exhibit resemblances among these languages.

- **Lexical Borrowings:** Throughout history, Dutch has borrowed vocabulary from other languages, notably Latin, French, and more recently, English. This linguistic borrowing enriches Dutch vocabulary and reflects historical and cultural influences.

Position within the Germanic Language Family:

- **West Germanic Branch:** Dutch is classified within the West Germanic branch, alongside other languages such as German, English, and Frisian. It is further divided into three main dialect groups: Low Franconian (spoken in the Netherlands and Flanders), Low German (spoken in northern Germany), and High German (spoken in Germany and Austria).

- **Mutual Intelligibility:** Dutch shares varying degrees of mutual intelligibility with other West Germanic languages, making it somewhat understandable for speakers of German and English, particularly in written form and basic conversations.

Language Evolution and Standardization:

- **Standard Dutch:** The modern standard form of Dutch, known as Algemeen Beschaafd Nederlands (ABN), emerged through the standardization of grammar, vocabulary, and pronunciation in the 19th and 20th centuries. This standardized version is used in education, media, and official communication in the Netherlands and Belgium.

There are many practical advantages to learning conversational Dutch, particularly for those who want to integrate into Dutch-speaking communities or negotiate daily life in Dutch-speaking regions. The importance of learning conversational Dutch goes beyond simple communication; it promotes cross-cultural understanding and eases relationships in a variety of contexts.

The Importance of Conversational Dutch

The practicality and benefits of learning conversational Dutch for day-to-day interactions and cultural integration.

There are many practical advantages to learning conversational Dutch, particularly for those who want to integrate into Dutch-speaking communities or negotiate daily life in Dutch-speaking regions. The importance of learning conversational Dutch goes beyond simple communication; it promotes cross-cultural understanding and eases relationships in a variety of contexts.

Practicality in Daily Interactions:

1. Social Interaction:

- **Networking:** Proficiency in conversational Dutch enables individuals to expand their social circles, fostering connections and friendships within the Dutch-speaking community.

- **Everyday Conversations:** From casual exchanges in shops, cafes, or public transport to more substantial conversations with neighbors or colleagues, conversational Dutch facilitates smoother interactions in everyday life.

2. Navigating Services:

- **Public Services:** Understanding Dutch helps in dealing with governmental institutions, healthcare services, and administrative procedures, ensuring better access to essential services.

- **Shopping and Daily Errands:** Being able to communicate effectively in Dutch is indispensable for activities such as grocery shopping, seeking assistance in stores, or navigating local services.

3. Employment Opportunities:

- **Job Prospects:** Proficiency in conversational Dutch significantly improves employment prospects, as many positions require at least a basic understanding of the language for effective communication in the workplace.

Cultural Integration:

1. Understanding the Culture:

- **Local Customs and Traditions:** Learning Dutch allows for a deeper understanding of Dutch culture, traditions, and societal norms, promoting a sense of belonging and cultural immersion.

- **Appreciation of Arts and Media:** Proficiency in the language grants access to a wide array of Dutch literature, films, and media, providing a richer cultural experience.

2. Integration and Acceptance:

- **Integration Efforts:** Speaking Dutch demonstrates a commitment to integrating into the local community, fostering acceptance and respect among locals.

- **Cultural Sensitivity:** Proficiency in the language facilitates cultural sensitivity and understanding, which are crucial elements in building meaningful relationships within the community.

Benefits Beyond Communication:

1. **Mental Stimulation:**

- Learning a new language stimulates cognitive functions, enhancing problem-solving skills, multitasking abilities, and overall mental agility.

2. **Personal Development:**

- **Confidence Boost:** Mastering conversational Dutch boosts confidence in social settings and enhances adaptability in diverse environments.

- **Cross-Cultural Competence:** It fosters a broader perspective, encouraging cross-cultural competence and empathy towards different cultural backgrounds.

Beyond just being able to communicate, conversational Dutch is essential for integrating into Dutch-speaking groups on a personal level, advancing culturally, and facilitating smooth daily interactions. Learning conversational Dutch is an investment that will benefit you in many ways, including increased practicality in a variety of contexts and a broader appreciation of Dutch language and culture.

Tips for Effective Language Learning

Setting realistic goals, creating study routines, and utilizing various learning resources.

Learning Dutch can be an enriching experience. Here are some effective tips tailored specifically for mastering the Dutch language:

Setting Realistic Goals:

1. Define Your Objectives:

- Determine why you want to learn Dutch—whether it's for travel, work, cultural appreciation, or personal interest.

- Set specific, achievable goals. For instance, aim to hold a basic conversation, understand news articles, or reach a certain proficiency level within a defined timeframe.

2. Break It Down:

- Divide your learning into smaller, manageable tasks. Focus on vocabulary, grammar, listening, speaking, and writing skills separately.

Creating Effective Study Routines:

1. Consistency Matters:

- Establish a consistent study schedule that fits your lifestyle. Short, regular study sessions are often more effective than infrequent, long ones.

- Dedicate time to practice listening, speaking, reading, and writing in Dutch during each study session.

2. Immersive Learning:

- Immerse yourself in the Dutch language and culture. Watch Dutch movies or series, listen to Dutch music or podcasts, and read books or news articles in Dutch.

- Label items in your environment with Dutch words to reinforce vocabulary.

3. Practice Speaking:

- Find language exchange partners or join Dutch-speaking communities to practice speaking. Engaging in conversations helps improve fluency and confidence.

Utilizing Learning Resources:

1. Language Learning Apps and Websites:

- Explore Dutch language apps like Babbel, Duolingo, or Rosetta Stone for structured lessons and interactive exercises.

- Websites such as Memrise or FluentU offer a variety of content to improve vocabulary, grammar, and listening skills.

2. Textbooks and Workbooks:

- Use Dutch textbooks or workbooks suitable for your proficiency level to reinforce grammar rules and practice exercises.

- Online resources like DutchGrammar.com or Learndutch.org provide explanations and exercises to improve grammar skills.

3. Seek Authentic Content:

- Read Dutch newspapers, blogs, or online articles to familiarize yourself with the language in real-life contexts.

- Watch Dutch TV shows, movies, or YouTube channels with subtitles to improve comprehension and pronunciation.

Additional Tips:

1. Keep a Dutch Journal:

- Practice writing by maintaining a journal in Dutch. Write about your day, thoughts, or experiences to improve your written skills.

2. Join Dutch Language Meetups:

- Attend language exchange events or Dutch-speaking meetups in your area or online. Interacting with native speakers enhances learning and cultural understanding.

3. Use Flashcards and Mnemonics:

- Create flashcards or use apps like Anki to memorize Dutch vocabulary. Mnemonics and visual aids can aid in retention.

4. Stay Persistent and Patient:

- Be patient with yourself; learning a new language takes time. Celebrate small victories and keep going even when facing challenges.

With consistent practice and integration of these tactics into your learning regimen, you will gradually improve your Dutch language proficiency. Being consistent, being committed, and exploring a variety of learning tools will definitely hasten your acquisition of Dutch language skills.

CHAPTER 2

Dutch Pronunciation and Phonetics

Dutch Alphabet and Sounds, Highlighting Unique Sounds and Letters

Basics of Dutch Pronunciation and Phonetics

Gaining a solid understanding of the fundamentals of Dutch phonetics and pronunciation is essential to learning the language. Although Dutch phonetics can be complex, learners can greatly benefit from breaking it down into its essential elements.

Here's an overview:

1. Vowel Sounds:

- Dutch vowels consist of both short and long sounds. For instance:

    - Short vowels: 'a' (as in 'kat' - cat), 'e' (as in 'pet' - pet), 'i' (as in 'kip' - chicken), 'o' (as in 'pot' - pot), 'u' (as in 'put' - pit)

    - Long vowels: 'aa' (as in 'vaar' - sail), 'ee' (as in 'veer' - feather), 'ie' (as in 'vlieg' - fly), 'oo' (as in 'boot' - boat), 'uu' (as in 'vuur' - fire)

2. Consonant Sounds:

- Some consonant sounds in Dutch might differ from English:

    - 'g' sound: A guttural sound produced at the back of the throat, similar to the 'ch' in Scottish 'loch' or the German 'ach'.

- 'r' sound: Pronounced with a rolling or trilled 'r', which might differ from the English 'r'.

- 'sch' sound: Often found in words like 'school', pronounced like 'sk' in English.

- 'ui' sound: A unique sound in Dutch, found in words like 'huis' (house), which can be challenging for non-native speakers.

3. Stress and Intonation:

- Dutch words generally follow a stress pattern, usually on the first syllable. However, some words might have stress on the second syllable or another syllable, depending on the word's structure and origin.

- Understanding and mimicking Dutch intonation patterns is crucial for sounding more natural and conveying meaning effectively.

4. Pronunciation Practice:

- Listening to native speakers and imitating their pronunciation helps in mastering the correct sounds and intonation.

- Using online resources, language apps, or language exchange groups for pronunciation practice can be beneficial.

- Regular practice of challenging sounds and words can aid in improvement.

5. Diphthongs and Digraphs:

- Dutch contains diphthongs (combinations of two vowel sounds in one syllable) and digraphs (two letters representing one sound), such as 'ei' (pronounced like 'ay' in English) and 'ou' (pronounced like 'ow' in English).

6. Accent Marks:

- Occasionally, accent marks (such as the diaeresis '¨') are used in Dutch to indicate the pronunciation of vowels in words like 'ë' (e.g., 'idee' - idea) or 'ü' (e.g., 'lingüïstiek' - linguistics).

7. Continuous Practice and Feedback:

- Consistent practice, receiving feedback, and making adjustments are crucial for improving pronunciation.

- Recording oneself speaking Dutch and comparing it to native speakers' pronunciation can aid in identifying areas for improvement.

Understanding and practicing Dutch pronunciation

and phonetics diligently can greatly enhance one's ability to speak the language fluently and communicate effectively with native speakers.

Pronunciation Guide

Detailed guidance on articulating Dutch sounds, stressing intonation, and stress patterns.

Although pronouncing words correctly in Dutch can be difficult, communication effectiveness depends on knowing the sounds and intonation patterns. This comprehensive guide can assist with pronouncing words in Dutch:

Dutch Vowel Sounds:

1. Short Vowels:

- **"A"**: Similar to the 'a' in "cat," but shorter and slightly more open.

- **"E"**: Pronounced like the 'e' in "bet."

- **"I"**: Similar to the 'i' in "sit."

- **"O"**: Sounds like the 'o' in "hot" but shorter.

- **"U"**: Closest to the 'u' in "put."

2. Long Vowels:

- **"AA"**: Sounds like the 'a' in "father" but longer.

- **"EE"**: Pronounced like the 'ay' in "say."

- **"OO"**: Similar to the 'o' in "go" but elongated.

- **"UU"**: Closest to the 'u' in "flute" but longer.

Dutch Consonant Sounds:

1. Guttural Sounds:

- **"G"**: Often a guttural sound, pronounced at the back of the throat. Similar to the 'ch' in the Scottish word "loch."

- **"CH"**: Similar to the 'g' in "loch" but softer in some words.

2. R Sounds:

- **"R"**: Usually a guttural or rolled 'r' sound, produced from the back of the throat or rolled at the tip of the tongue.

3. Sibilant Sounds:

- **"S"**: Typically pronounced as a sharp 's' sound, similar to the English 's.'

- **"Z"**: Sounds like the 'z' in "zero."

Intonation and Stress Patterns:

1. Word Stress:

- In Dutch, stress usually falls on the first syllable of the word. Practice recognizing and placing emphasis on the correct syllable in words.

2. Sentence Intonation:

- Dutch generally has a fairly flat intonation compared to some other languages. Sentences often end with a downward intonation, especially in declarative statements.

Tips for Practicing Pronunciation:

1. Listen and Repeat:

- Listen to native speakers and imitate their pronunciation. Mimic the sounds, intonation, and stress patterns.

2. Use Pronunciation Guides:

- Utilize online resources, pronunciation guides, or language learning apps with audio recordings to practice correct pronunciation.

3. Record Yourself:

- Record yourself speaking Dutch and compare it with native pronunciation. This helps identify areas needing improvement.

4. Work with a Tutor or Language Partner:

- Engage with a Dutch tutor or language partner who can provide guidance and correct your pronunciation.

5. Practice Tongue Twisters and Rhymes:

- Tongue twisters and rhymes in Dutch can help you practice specific sounds and improve your overall pronunciation.

6. Be Patient and Persistent:

- Pronunciation may take time to master. Be patient with yourself, and keep practicing regularly.

Focusing on vowels, consonants, intonation, and stress patterns will help you gradually get better at pronouncing words correctly and increase your capacity for efficient Dutch communication. Your progress will be greatly aided by exposure to native speakers and regular practice.

Common Pronunciation Mistakes and How to Avoid Them

The distinctive sounds and phonetic nuances of Dutch can make pronunciation difficult to master. Learners can greatly benefit from knowing common pronunciation errors and how to correct them to speak more accurately and confidently. The following are some common mistakes made by students, along with solutions:

1. Difficulty with Guttural 'G' Sound:

- **Mistake:** Non-native speakers often struggle with pronouncing the guttural 'g', producing a sound closer to the English 'g'.

- **Solution:** Practice producing the sound by making a throaty, raspy sound similar to clearing your throat. Mimic native speakers and practice words like 'goed' (good) or 'geel' (yellow) to refine the pronunciation.

2. Mispronunciation of 'R':

- **Mistake:** Some learners may find it challenging to roll or trill the Dutch 'r' sound, often substituting it with the English 'r'.

- **Solution:** Practice the rolling 'r' sound by flicking the tip of your tongue against the roof of your mouth. Mimic native speakers and repeat words like 'rood' (red) or 'regen' (rain) to improve pronunciation.

3. Vowel Sounds and Diphthongs:

- **Mistake:** Misplacing emphasis or mispronouncing Dutch vowel sounds and diphthongs.

- **Solution:** Focus on distinguishing between short and long vowels, as well as practicing diphthongs. Use resources that break down these sounds and offer exercises to practice their correct pronunciation.

4. Neglecting Word Stress and Intonation:

- **Mistake:** Incorrectly placing stress on syllables or not following Dutch intonation patterns.

- **Solution:** Listen to native speakers to understand their stress and intonation patterns. Pay attention to the rhythm of the language and practice speaking sentences with the appropriate stress.

5. Lack of Feedback and Correction:

- **Mistake:** Learners might not receive enough feedback or correction on their pronunciation.

- **Solution:** Engage with native speakers or language instructors who can provide constructive feedback. Utilize language exchange groups or platforms where you can practice speaking and receive guidance.

6. Avoiding Practice and Consistency:

- **Mistake:** Insufficient and irregular practice may hinder progress in improving pronunciation.

- **Solution:** Dedicate regular time for pronunciation practice. Utilize resources such as language apps, online videos, or audiobooks that focus specifically on pronunciation drills and exercises.

7. Not Emulating Native Speakers:

- **Mistake:** Failing to mimic the speech patterns, rhythm, and intonation of native Dutch speakers.

- **Solution:** Listen to native Dutch content like

podcasts, movies, or music. Try to imitate their pronunciation and rhythm to assimilate natural speech patterns.

Through the identification of frequent pronunciation problems and the implementation of intentional tactics to overcome them, learners can achieve notable progress in their ability to pronounce Dutch words accurately and confidently. Substantial progress can be achieved over time with regular practice, exposure to native speech, and concentration on particular difficulty areas.

Practice Drills and Exercises for Pronunciation Improvement and Reinforcement

It takes regular practice and focused activities to reinforce proper articulation and intonation when learning how to pronounce Dutch words correctly. The following practice tasks are intended to help students improve their pronunciation:

1. Minimal Pair Practice:

- **Objective:** Focus on distinguishing between similar sounds that may cause confusion.

- **Exercise:** Practice pairs of words that differ by only one sound (minimal pairs), such as 'kat' (cat) and 'ket' (chain). Repeat these words, emphasizing the distinct sounds to sharpen your ability to discern subtle differences.

2. Tongue Twisters:

- **Objective:** Enhance speech fluency and accuracy by mastering challenging combinations of sounds and syllables.

- **Exercise:** Practice Dutch tongue twisters, such as "De kat krabt de krullen van de trap" (The cat scratches the curls off the stairs). Repeatedly recite these phrases slowly at first, gradually increasing speed while maintaining accuracy.

3. Recording and Self-Evaluation:

- **Objective:** Assess your own pronunciation and identify areas for improvement.

- **Exercise:** Record yourself speaking Dutch phrases or sentences. Compare your pronunciation to native speakers or pronunciation guides. Listen for differences and work on adjusting your speech accordingly.

4. Vowel and Consonant Drills:

- **Objective:** Focus on specific vowel or consonant sounds that present difficulties.

- **Exercise:** Create drills that isolate challenging sounds. For instance, practice repeating a series of words containing the 'ui' sound ('huis', 'luid', 'muis') or focus solely on the guttural 'g' sound ('goed', 'geel', 'gang').

5. Reading Aloud and Shadowing:

- **Objective:** Improve rhythm, intonation, and natural speech flow.

- **Exercise:** Read Dutch texts or passages aloud, paying attention to stress, rhythm, and intonation. Shadowing involves listening to a native speaker and repeating what they say immediately after, mimicking their pronunciation and intonation.

6. Interactive Pronunciation Apps and Websites:

- **Objective:** Utilize technology for interactive and targeted pronunciation practice.

- **Exercise:** Explore language learning apps or websites offering pronunciation exercises, interactive drills, and feedback mechanisms designed to improve Dutch pronunciation.

7. Conversation Practice with Native Speakers:

- **Objective:** Apply learned pronunciation skills in real-life scenarios.

- **Exercise:** Engage in conversations with native Dutch speakers through language exchange programs or conversation groups. Request feedback on your pronunciation and actively work on improving based on their suggestions.

8. Enlist a Language Partner or Tutor:

- **Objective:** Receive personalized guidance and correction from an experienced speaker.

- **Exercise:** Partner with a native Dutch speaker, tutor, or language exchange partner who can provide targeted exercises and feedback to refine your pronunciation skills.[1]

The keys to successfully improving your Dutch pronunciation are exposure to native speech, focused exercises, and consistent practice. Through the integration of these exercises into your learning regimen, you will be able to progressively improve your accuracy and confidence when pronouncing Dutch sounds.

---

1. Complete Dutch Beginner to Intermediate Course: Learn to read, write, speak and understand a new language with Teach Yourself – Dennis Strik and Gerdi Quist

CHAPTER 3

Essential Vocabulary and Phrases

Common Greetings, Introductions, and Polite Expressions

Learning common greetings, introductions, and polite expressions in Dutch is essential for effective communication and building rapport in social interactions. Here's how to become proficient in these core areas of

Dutch language and culture:

1. Basic Greetings:

- **"Hallo" or "Hoi":** These are casual ways to say "hello" in Dutch.

- **"Goedemorgen":** Meaning "good morning."

- **"Goedemiddag":** Translating to "good afternoon."

- **"Goedenavond":** Used to say "good evening."

2. Introducing Yourself:

- **"Ik heet..." or "Mijn naam is...":** These phrases mean "My name is..." when introducing yourself.

- **"Aangenaam kennis te maken":** Translating to "Nice to meet you."

3. Formal and Informal Address:

- **"U" and "Jij/Je":** "U" is the formal way to address someone, while "Jij" or "Je" is more informal and used among peers or in familiar settings.

4. Polite Expressions:

- **"Dank je wel" or "Bedankt":** These mean "thank you" in Dutch.

- **"Alsjeblieft" or "Alstublieft":** Translating to "please" or "here you go" in different contexts (informal/formal).

5. Asking How Someone is Doing:

- **"Hoe gaat het?" or "Hoe gaat het met jou?":** Meaning "How are you?" in Dutch.

- **"Het gaat goed" or "Het gaat prima":** These responses convey "I'm doing well" or "I'm doing fine."

6. Farewells:

- **"Tot ziens":** Equivalent to "goodbye" or "see you soon" in Dutch.

- **"Dag" or "Tot later":** Casual ways to say "bye" or "see you later."

7. Cultural Considerations:

- **Handshakes:** In formal settings or when meeting someone for the first time, a handshake is common. Use a firm handshake while making eye contact.

- **Respecting Personal Space:** Dutch people value their personal space, so maintain a comfortable distance when interacting.

8. Practice Scenarios:

- **Role-Playing:** Engage in role-playing exercises to simulate everyday greeting and introduction scenarios. Practice using these expressions in different contexts.

9. Listening and Repetition:

- **Audio Resources:** Listen to native speakers or audio materials to familiarize yourself with the correct pronunciation and intonation of greetings and introductions.

- **Repeat and Mimic:** Repetition is key to mastering pronunciation. Practice repeating greetings and introductions until you feel comfortable with the sounds and rhythm.

10. Real-Life Application:

- **Use in Daily Interactions:** Apply these greetings and introductions in real-life situations, such as meeting new people, shopping, or interacting with locals, to reinforce your learning.

Learning how to say hello, introduce yourself, and use polite expressions in Dutch shows respect for Dutch social standards and culture while also facilitating easy communication. You will feel more at ease and secure utilizing these expressions in casual discussions if you practice them frequently and are exposed to them in a variety of settings.

Cardinal and Ordinal Numbers, Telling Time, and Expressing Dates

Comprehending numbers, time, and dates in Dutch is essential for daily correspondence and appointment scheduling. This is a thorough guide to learning certain Dutch language skills:

1. Cardinal Numbers (1-10):

- "één" (1), "twee" (2), "drie" (3), "vier" (4), "vijf" (5), "zes" (6), "zeven" (7), "acht" (8), "negen" (9), "tien" (10).

2. Ordinal Numbers:

- "eerste" (1st), "tweede" (2nd), "derde" (3rd), "vierde" (4th), "vijfde" (5th), "zesde" (6th), "zevende" (7th), "achtste" (8th), "negende" (9th), "tiende" (10th).

3. Larger Numbers:

- **Learn the pattern:** Once you've mastered the numbers 1-10, understanding larger numbers follows a pattern. For example, 11 is "elf," 12 is "twaalf," and so on.

4. Telling Time:

- **"Hoe laat is het?":** Meaning "What time is it?"

- **"Het is... uur":** Use this phrase when telling time, followed by the hour (e.g., "Het is twee uur" - It is two o'clock).

- **"Kwart over...":** Indicates a quarter past the hour (e.g., "Het is kwart over drie" - It is a quarter past three).

- **"Half...":** Refers to half past the hour (e.g., "Het is half vier" - It is half past three).

- **"Kwart voor...":** Means a quarter to the next hour (e.g., "Het is kwart voor vijf" - It is a quarter to five).

5. Days of the Week:

- "Maandag" (Monday), "Dinsdag" (Tuesday), "Woensdag" (Wednesday), "Donderdag" (Thursday), "Vrijdag" (Friday), "Zaterdag" (Saturday), "Zondag" (Sunday).

6. Months:

- "Januari" (January), "Februari" (February), "Maart" (March), "April" (April), "Mei" (May), "Juni" (June), "Juli" (July), "Augustus" (August), "September" (September), "Oktober" (October), "November" (November), "December" (December).

7. Expressing Dates:

- "Vandaag" (Today), "Morgen" (Tomorrow), "Gisteren" (Yesterday).

- **"Het is de..."**: To express the date (e.g., "Het is de vijfde juni" - It is the fifth of June).

- **Format:** In Dutch, the date format often follows the day, month, year sequence (e.g., 5 juni 2023).

8. Practice and Application:

- **Practice Exercises:** Create exercises to practice saying dates, telling time, and using numbers in various contexts.

- **Daily Use:** Apply your knowledge in daily life by asking and telling the time, scheduling appointments, and discussing dates with native speakers or language partners.

Gaining proficiency in Dutch with numbers, time, and dates is essential for efficient scheduling, communication, and comprehension of temporal references in discourse. Your competence in these core language concepts will be cemented with frequent practice and immersion in real-world situations.

Basic Conversational Phrases for Everyday Situations Like Shopping, Dining, and Traveling

Acquiring rudimentary conversational Dutch phrases for commonplace circumstances such as dining, shopping, and travel will significantly improve your ability to navigate various scenarios.

Here is a list of essential expressions for these situations:

1. Shopping:

- **"Hoeveel kost dit?"** - How much does this cost?

- **"Ik wil graag betalen."** - I would like to pay.

- **"Heeft u dit in een andere kleur?"** - Do you have this in another color?

- **"Mag ik een bonnetje alstublieft?"** - Can I have a receipt, please?

- "Ik zoek..." - I'm looking for...

- "Kunt u mij helpen?" - Can you help me?

2. Dining:

- "Een tafel voor twee alstublieft." - A table for two, please.

- "Mag ik de menukaart zien?" - Can I see the menu?

- "Ik wil graag bestellen." - I would like to order.

- "Kunt u de rekening brengen?" - Could you bring the bill?

- "Dit smaakt heerlijk!" - This tastes delicious!

- "Graag apart betalen." - Separate checks, please.

3. Traveling:

- "Waar is het treinstation/vliegveld?" - Where is the train station/airport?

- "Ik zoek een hotel." - I'm looking for a hotel.

- "Hoe kom ik bij...?" - How do I get to...?

- "Mag ik een kaartje, alstublieft?" - Can I have

a ticket, please?

- **"Kunt u mij helpen met mijn bagage?"** - Can you help me with my luggage?

- **"Hoe laat vertrekt de bus/trein?"** - What time does the bus/train depart?

4. General Conversational Phrases:

- **"Dank je wel" / "Bedankt"** - Thank you.

- **"Alsjeblieft" / "Alstublieft"** - Please/Here you go.

- **"Excuseer" / "Pardon"** - Excuse me.

- **"Sorry"** - Sorry.

- **"Ja" / "Nee"** - Yes / No.

- **"Ik begrijp het niet."** - I don't understand.

5. Emergency Situations:

- **"Bel alstublieft de politie/ambulance."** - Please call the police/ambulance.

- **"Ik heb hulp nodig."** - I need help.

- **"Kunt u mij helpen? Ik spreek geen Nederlands."** - Can you help me? I don't speak Dutch.

- **"Waar is het dichtstbijzijnde ziekenhuis?"** - Where is the nearest hospital?

Your confidence and capacity to successfully communicate in Dutch in a variety of everyday circumstances will be greatly enhanced by practicing these phrases and applying them to role-playing scenarios or everyday conversations.

Essential Vocabulary for Everyday Situations and Practical Communication

This is a compilation of key words for everyday Dutch conversations that cover a range of real-world scenarios:

1. At Home:

- **"Huis"** - House

- **"Slaapkamer"** - Bedroom

- **"Badkamer"** - Bathroom

- **"Keuken"** - Kitchen

- **"Woonkamer"** - Living room

- **"Bank"** - Sofa/Couch

- **"Tafel"** - Table

- **"Stoel"** - Chair

- **"Koelkast"** - Refrigerator

- **"Bed"** - Bed

2. Food and Dining:

- **"Eten"** - Food

- **"Drinken"** - Drink

- **"Ontbijt"** - Breakfast

- **"Lunch"** - Lunch

- **"Diner"** - Dinner

- **"Brood"** - Bread

- **"Groenten"** - Vegetables

- **"Fruit"** - Fruit

- **"Vlees"** - Meat

- **"Vis"** - Fish

3. Shopping:

- **"Winkel"** - Shop/Store

- **"Kleding"** - Clothes

- **"Schoenen"** - Shoes

- **"Tassen"** - Bags

- **"Boeken"** - Books

- **"Elektronica"** - Electronics

- **"Sieraden"** - Jewelry

- **"Cosmetica"** - Cosmetics

- **"Geld"** - Money

4. Transportation:

- **"Auto"** - Car

- **"Bus"** - Bus

- **"Trein"** - Train

- **"Fiets"** - Bicycle

- **"Taxi"** - Taxi

- **"Station"** - Station

- **"Halte"** - Stop

- **"Kaartje"** - Ticket

- **"Bagage"** - Luggage

5. Health and Emergencies:

- **"Ziekenhuis"** - Hospital

- **"Dokter"** - Doctor

- **"Apotheek"** - Pharmacy

- **"Hulp"** - Help

- **"Noodgeval"** - Emergency

- **"Ambulance"** - Ambulance

- **"Brandweer"** - Fire department

- **"Politie"** - Police

6. Daily Activities:

- **"Werken"** - Work

- **"Studeren"** - Study

- **"Sporten"** - Exercise/Sports

- **"Ontspannen"** - Relax

- **"Slapen"** - Sleep

- **"Spelen"** - Play

- **"Kijken"** - Watch/Look

7. Time and Dates:

- **"Tijd"** - Time

- **"Uur"** - Hour

- **"Dag"** - Day

- **"Week"** - Week

- **"Maand"** - Month

- **"Jaar"** - Year

- **"Vandaag"** - Today

- **"Morgen"** - Tomorrow

- **"Gisteren"** - Yesterday[1]

You can substantially improve your ability to speak successfully in Dutch in a variety of everyday scenarios by learning and using these vocabulary words in context. Regular use and exposure to these terminologies can help you become more confident and proficient in the language.

1. Easy Dutch Phrase Book: Over 1500 Common Phrases For Everyday Use And Travel – By Lingo Mastery

CHAPTER 4

Basic Grammar and Sentence Structure

Dutch Gendered Nouns and Their Respective Articles

Nouns in Dutch are gendered, and their gender determines which articles ("the" or "a/an") are used with them. An overview of gendered nouns in Dutch and the articles that go with them is provided below:

1. Gender in Dutch Nouns:

- Dutch nouns are divided into three genders: masculine (de), feminine (de), and neuter (het).

- Unlike languages like French or German, where gender is often based on the actual gender of the object, Dutch gender is not always predictable and has to be learned with each noun.

2. Definite Articles (The):

- **Masculine (de):** For masculine nouns, the definite article "the" is "de." For example, "de man" (the man), "de tafel" (the table).

- **Feminine (de):** Feminine nouns also use "de" as the definite article. For instance, "de vrouw" (the woman), "de stoel" (the chair).

- **Neuter (het):** Neuter nouns take the definite article "het." For example, "het huis" (the house), "het boek" (the book).

3. Indefinite Articles (A/An):

- **Masculine (een):** The indefinite article "a/an" for masculine nouns is "een." For instance, "een man" (a man), "een tafel" (a table).

- **Feminine (een):** Feminine nouns also use "een" as the indefinite article. For example, "een vrouw" (a woman), "een stoel" (a chair).

- **Neuter (een):** Neuter nouns also take "een" as the indefinite article. For instance, "een huis" (a house), "een boek" (a book).

4. Learning Gender:

- Unfortunately, there are no strict rules for determining the gender of Dutch nouns. The gender often needs to be memorized along with the noun itself.

- Some general tendencies exist, such as words ending in "-heid" (feminine) or "-je" (neuter) often being associated with specific genders, but these are not absolute rules.

5. Plurals:

- In Dutch, plurals are formed by adding "-en" or "-s" to the singular form of the noun. For example, "mannen" (men), "tafels" (tables), "huizen" (houses).

6. Practice and Exposure:

- Consistent exposure to Dutch language materials and regular practice with nouns, using their correct articles, is key to mastering gendered nouns in Dutch.

- Pay attention to the gender of nouns while learning vocabulary and use them in sentences to reinforce proper usage.

It is essential to comprehend the gender of nouns and the articles that go with them in order to construct grammatically sound Dutch sentences. Your ability to utilize gendered nouns effectively in Dutch will progressively improve with practice and exposure, even though it may seem complicated at first.

The Basics of Verb Conjugation in the Present Tense

Comprehending present tense verb conjugation is essential for building sentences and speaking well in Dutch. The fundamentals of present tense verb conjugation are explained as follows:

1. Regular Verbs:

- In Dutch, regular verbs in the present tense follow a relatively straightforward pattern based on the subject pronouns (I, you, he/she/it, we, you, they).

- Let's take the verb "lopen" (to walk) as an example:

Subject Pronoun

Verb "Lopen" (to walk)

Ik (I)

loop

Jij (You)

loopt

Hij/Zij/Het (He/She/It)

loopt

Wij (We)

lopen

Jullie (You all)

lopen

Zij (They)

lopen

2. Irregular Verbs:

- Some Dutch verbs are irregular and do not follow the standard conjugation patterns.

- For instance, the verb "zijn" (to be) is irregular:

Subject Pronoun

Verb "Zijn" (to be)

Ik (I)

ben

Jij (You)

bent

Hij/Zij/Het (He/She/It)

is

Wij (We)

zijn

Jullie (You all)

zijn

Zij (They)

zijn

3. Stem-changing Verbs:

- Some verbs undergo stem changes (vowel changes) in the present tense for specific subject pronouns.

- For example, the verb "eten" (to eat) changes its stem from "e" to "i" for subject pronouns "hij/zij/het" (he/she/it):

Subject Pronoun

Verb "Eten" (to eat)

Hij/Zij/Het (He/She/It)

eet

4. Practice and Application:

- Regular practice with verb conjugation charts and exercises will help reinforce the patterns and irregularities in verb forms.

- Use verbs in sentences to practice their conjugation in different contexts and with various subject pronouns.

For Dutch phrases to make sense, it is essential to grasp present-tense verb conjugation. You can become more proficient at utilizing verbs in the present tense by practicing frequently, being exposed to verbs in different settings, and employing them in discussions regularly.

Forming Simple Sentences and Questions

Understanding fundamental sentence structure and word order is necessary to form simple phrases and queries in Dutch. Here's a guide to help you construct uncomplicated sentences and questions:

1. Basic Sentence Structure:

- In Dutch, the basic word order for simple sentences is Subject-Verb-Object (SVO), similar to English.

- For instance: "Ik (subject) lees (verb) een boek (object)" translates to "I read a book."

2. Subject Pronouns:

- Common subject pronouns include "Ik" (I), "Jij" (You), "Hij" (He), "Zij" (She), "Het" (It), "Wij" (We), "Jullie" (You all), "Zij" (They).

- Place the subject pronoun at the beginning of the sentence to indicate who is performing the action.

3. Verbs and Conjugation:

- Conjugate verbs according to the subject pronoun and the tense (present, past, future, etc.).

- Use the correct verb form that matches the subject pronoun in the sentence.

4. Objects and Nouns:

- Objects or nouns come after the verb in a sentence.

- For example: "Ik eet een appel" (I eat an apple).

5. Forming Questions:

- In Dutch, to form a question, invert the subject and verb. There is no auxiliary verb like "do" in English.

- For example: "Jij spreekt Engels" (You speak English) becomes "Spreek jij Engels?" (Do you speak English?).

6. Question Words:

- Use question words like "Wie" (Who), "Wat" (What), "Waar" (Where), "Wanneer" (When), "Waarom" (Why), "Hoe" (How) at the beginning of a question to inquire about specific information.

- For instance: "Wat is dat?" (What is that?), "Waar is de bibliotheek?" (Where is the library?).

7. Practice and Application:

- Practice forming simple sentences by combining subject pronouns, verbs, and objects.

- Experiment with different verbs and objects to create varied sentences.

- Practice asking and answering questions using question words to inquire about specific details.

Example Sentences:

- "Ik ga naar school" (I go to school).

- "Jij leest een boek" (You read a book).

- "Hij speelt voetbal" (He plays soccer).

- "Zij drinkt water" (She drinks water).

- "Wij eten pizza" (We eat pizza).

- "Spreek jij Nederlands?" (Do you speak Dutch?).[1]

Forming simple phrases and questions in Dutch requires an understanding of sentence structure, the use of question words, proper verb conjugation, and appropriate subject pronouns. Applying and practicing these concepts consistently will improve your Dutch communication skills.

Building Basic Conversations

Constructing and practicing basic dialogues

Establishing fundamental dialogues is an essential phase in learning Dutch, since it enables students to utilize their language abilities in real-world situations. Here's a guide to engaging learners in constructing and practicing basic dialogues:

1. Select a Theme:

- Choose a theme or context for the conversation, such as introducing oneself, ordering food, discussing hobbies, or asking for directions.

2. Identify Key Vocabulary and Phrases:

- Compile relevant vocabulary and phrases related to the chosen theme. For instance, if the theme is ordering food, include words and expressions like "menu," "eten" (food), "drinken" (drink), "bestellen" (to order), and phrases like "Ik wil graag..." (I would like...), "Mag ik de kaart?" (Can I have the menu?).

3. Create Dialogue Templates:

- Develop simple dialogue templates that incorporate the identified vocabulary and phrases. For instance:

  - Dialogue 1: Ordering Food

    - Person A: "Goedemiddag, mag ik de menukaart alstublieft?"

    - Person B: "Natuurlijk, alstublieft. Wat wilt u bestellen?"

    - Person A: "Ik wil graag een pizza Margherita en een glas water, alstublieft."

4. Role-Play Exercises:

- Assign roles to learners and encourage them to practice the dialogues in pairs or small groups.

- Rotate roles to allow each participant to experience both sides of the conversation.

5. Add Variation and Expand Dialogues:

- Once learners are comfortable with the basic dialogue, introduce variations. For example, change the order or add new vocabulary to expand the conversation.

- Include responses to possible questions or reactions to make the dialogue more dynamic and realistic.

6. Encourage Contextual Practice:

- Prompt learners to apply the dialogues in real or simulated situations. For instance, simulate a restaurant scenario where learners order food or a role-play involving asking for directions.

7. Provide Feedback and Correction:

- Offer constructive feedback on pronunciation, grammar, and vocabulary usage to help learners improve their conversation skills.

- Encourage learners to ask questions and seek clarification on language aspects they find challenging.

8. Utilize Multimedia Resources:

- Use audio recordings, videos, or online platforms with native speakers engaging in similar conversations to provide examples and reinforce learning.

9. Recap and Reinforce:

- Review the learned dialogues regularly to reinforce vocabulary and sentence structures.[2]

- Encourage learners to practice outside of class by engaging in conversations with peers or practicing with language exchange partners.

Scaffolding vocabulary, rehearsing dialogues, role-playing, and using acquired abilities in authentic situations are all necessary to build fundamental conversations in Dutch. Through methodical practice and a step-by-step increase in interaction, students can become more comfortable and proficient in conducting basic Dutch discussions.

---

1. Conversational Dutch Dialogues: Over 100 Dutch Conversations and Short Stories – by Lingo Mastery

2. Conversational Dutch Dialogues: Over 100 Dutch Conversations and Short Stories – by Lingo Mastery

CHAPTER 5

Expanding Conversational Skill

Past and Future Tenses,
Expanding on Verb Conjugation
and Sentence Structures

Gaining proficiency in Dutch's past and future tenses will improve your capacity to communicate events that have happened or will occur in the future. This is introduction to intermediate grammar with an emphasis on sentence patterns, verb conjugation, and past and future tenses:

1. Past Tense (Verleden Tijd):

- In Dutch, the past tense is formed differently for regular and irregular verbs.

Regular Verbs:

- Regular verbs in the past tense are formed by adding '-de' or '-te' to the verb stem, depending on the verb ending.

- For example, "werken" (to work) becomes "ik werkte" (I worked), and "spelen" (to play) becomes "jij speelde" (you played).

Irregular Verbs:

- Irregular verbs have unique past tense forms that don't follow a specific pattern.

- For example, "zijn" (to be) changes to "ik was" (I was), "hebben" (to have) becomes "ik had" (I had), etc.

2. Future Tense (Toekomende Tijd):

- The future tense in Dutch is often formed using the auxiliary verb "zullen" (shall/will) followed by the infinitive of the main verb.

- For example, "Ik zal werken" (I will work), "Jij zult eten" (You will eat).

3. Modal Verbs in Future Tense:

- Modal verbs like "kunnen" (can), "mogen" (may), "moeten" (must), and "willen" (want) can also express the future tense.

- For instance, "Ik kan het doen" (I can do it), "Hij wil morgen komen" (He wants to come tomorrow).

4. Sentence Structures in Past and Future Tenses:

- The basic word order in sentences remains the same in past and future tenses as in the present tense: Subject-Verb-Object.

- For instance, "Hij heeft gisteren een boek gelezen" (He read a book yesterday), "Wij zullen morgen naar Amsterdam gaan" (We will go to Amsterdam tomorrow).

5. Practice and Application:

- Practice verb conjugation for past and future tenses with regular and irregular verbs.

- Formulate sentences or short narratives using past and future tenses to describe past events or future plans.

6. Adverbs of Time:

- Incorporate adverbs of time (yesterday, tomorrow, last week, next year) to indicate when actions took place or will take place.

- For example, "Vorige maand ben ik naar Parijs gereisd" (Last month, I traveled to Paris), "Volgende zomer ga ik op vakantie" (Next summer, I am going on vacation).

Gaining proficiency in past and future tenses will improve your capacity to communicate in Dutch over time. Your understanding of past and future verb conjugations and sentence constructions will become more firm with regular practice, exposure to a variety of texts, and consistent application of these tenses in writing and speech.

Vocabulary and Phrases for Expressing Personal Opinions, Desires, and Needs

Effective communication in a variety of contexts is made possible by the ability to express thoughts, wants, and desires in Dutch. The following list of words and expressions can be used to express individual needs, wants, and opinions:

1. Expressing Opinions:

- "Ik denk dat..." - I think that...

- "Naar mijn mening..." - In my opinion...

- "Volgens mij..." - According to me...

- "Ik ben van mening dat..." - I am of the opinion that...

- "Het lijkt mij dat..." - It seems to me that...

- "Ik vind dat..." - I find that...

2. Stating Desires:

- "Ik wil graag..." - I would like...

- "Ik zou willen..." - I would want to...

- "Ik hoop dat..." - I hope that...

- "Ik verlang naar..." - I long for...

- "Ik wens..." - I wish...

3. Expressing Needs:

- "Ik heb... nodig." - I need...

- "Ik moet..." - I must...

- **"Kan ik alsjeblieft..."** - Can I please...

- **"Ik zou graag hulp willen met..."** - I would like help with...

- **"Ik zoek..."** - I am looking for...

4. Specific Vocabulary:

- **"Eten"** - Food

- **"Drinken"** - Drink

- **"Huisvesting"** - Housing

- **"Onderwijs"** - Education

- **"Gezondheidszorg"** - Healthcare

- **"Vervoer"** - Transportation

- **"Assistentie"** - Assistance

- **"Informatie"** - Information

- **"Hulp"** - Help

5. Phrases for Requesting Assistance:

- **"Kunt u mij alsjeblieft helpen?"** - Can you please help me?

- **"Zou u mij kunnen adviseren?"** - Could you

advise me?

- **"Kunt u mij alstublieft uitleggen..."** - Could you please explain to me...

- **"Kan ik om uw hulp vragen?"** - Can I ask for your help?

- **"Ik heb dringend hulp nodig."** - I urgently need help.

6. Polite Expressions:

- **"Alsjeblieft"** - Please

- **"Dank je wel"** / **"Bedankt"** - Thank you

- **"Alstublieft"** - Here you go/Please

- **"Excuseer"** / **"Pardon"** - Excuse me

- **"Sorry"** - Sorry[1]

By using these words and phrases, you will be able to express your requirements, wants, and opinions in Dutch-speaking settings. To improve your communication abilities, always remember to modify your vocabulary to fit the formality of the circumstance and use these expressions in a variety of settings.

Conversational Strategies and Techniques

Strategies to maintain and steer conversations effectively.

To effectively maintain and guide conversations in Dutch, one must become proficient in conversational methods and procedures.

The following techniques will assist you in navigating conversations:

1. Active Listening:

- **Engage Actively:** Show interest by nodding, maintaining eye contact, and using verbal cues like "ja" (yes) or "inderdaad" (indeed) to indicate understanding.

- **Paraphrase:** Reflect back what you've heard to confirm understanding. For example, "Dus, je bedoelt dat..." (So, you mean that...).

2. Asking Open-Ended Questions:

- **Encourage Elaboration:** Use questions starting with "Wat," "Waarom," "Hoe," or "Wanneer" (What, Why, How, When) to prompt detailed responses.

- **Example:** "Wat vind je het leukst aan je werk?" (What do you like most about your job?)

3. Providing Affirmation and Agreement:

- **Validate Responses:** Use affirmations like "Ja, dat begrijp ik" (Yes, I understand) or "Dat klinkt interessant" (That sounds interesting) to show support and agreement.

4. Steering the Conversation:

- **Transition Smoothly:** Use transition phrases like "Overigens" (By the way), "Daarnaast" (Additionally), or "Even terugkomend op..." (Going back to...) to guide the conversation in a certain direction.

- **Redirecting:** Politely steer the conversation towards a different topic by introducing related points.

5. Showing Interest and Empathy:

- **Express Empathy:** Use phrases like "Dat moet moeilijk zijn geweest" (That must have been difficult) or "Ik begrijp hoe je je voelt" (I understand how you feel) to demonstrate empathy and understanding.

6. Clarification and Confirmation:

- **Ask for Clarification:** If you're unsure, politely ask for clarification using phrases like "Bedoel je dat...?" (Do you mean that...?) or "Kun je dat uitleggen?" (Could you explain that?).

- **Confirm Understanding:** Summarize key points or repeat information to ensure mutual understanding.

7. Balancing Participation:

- **Avoid Dominating:** Be mindful of allowing others to contribute. Avoid monopolizing the conversation and ensure everyone has a chance to speak.

- **Encourage Others:** Encourage quieter participants by asking for their opinions or thoughts.

8. Responding to Challenges:

- **Handling Disagreements:** Stay respectful; use phrases like "Ik begrijp je standpunt, maar..." (I understand your point of view, but...) to express disagreements politely.

- **De-escalate Conflicts:** Stay calm and seek common ground if conflicts arise.

9. Cultural Awareness:

- **Respect Cultural Norms:** Be aware of cultural nuances in communication styles and adapt your approach accordingly.

Not only will using these conversational methods and techniques improve your Dutch communication abilities, but they will also help you have more meaningful and interesting conversations. For effective communication, put these strategies into regular practice and modify them according to various social settings.

Role-Playing Exercises and Dialogues

Engaging in role-play scenarios to practice new skills.

Role-playing exercises and conversations are great ways to get students interested in using and developing their Dutch language skills. By encouraging active engagement and simulating real-life settings, these exercises improve communication skills. Here's a guide to engaging learners in role-play exercises:

1. Select Relevant Scenarios:

- Choose scenarios relevant to learners' interests or daily life, such as ordering food at a restaurant, buying tickets, job interviews, or asking for directions.

2. Create Dialogue Scripts:

- Develop dialogue scripts outlining roles, interactions, and key phrases for each participant. Ensure that dialogues incorporate target vocabulary and grammatical structures.

3. Assign Roles:

- Assign specific roles or characters to participants. Distribute role cards outlining their character's background, intentions, and necessary information for the scenario.

4. Practice the Scenarios:

- Encourage participants to rehearse their dialogues, focusing on pronunciation, intonation, and fluency.

- Provide opportunities for participants to familiarize themselves with their roles and dialogue content.

5. Role-Playing Sessions:

- Conduct role-playing sessions where participants act out their assigned roles, engage in conversations based on the scenario, and apply learned language skills.

- Encourage improvisation and realistic interactions to simulate authentic situations.

6. Feedback and Discussion:

- After each role-play session, facilitate discussions. Provide constructive feedback on language use, communication effectiveness, and areas for improvement.

- Encourage participants to reflect on their experiences and discuss challenges faced during the role-play.

7. Rotate Roles:

- Rotate roles among participants to offer everyone a chance to play different characters and experience varied perspectives within the scenario.

8. Variation and Complexity:

- Gradually increase the complexity of scenarios by introducing new vocabulary, grammar structures, or challenging situations.

- Incorporate diverse scenarios to broaden participants' language repertoire.

9. Encourage Creativity and Flexibility:

- Encourage participants to be creative and adaptable during role-play exercises, allowing room for spontaneity and improvisation.

10. Practical Application:

- Encourage participants to apply the language skills acquired from role-playing sessions in real-life situations, reinforcing their learning.

Dutch role-playing exercises provide an engaging and participatory method of language learning, allowing students to hone their language abilities in a real-world setting. Participants can improve their fluency, confidence, and capacity for successful communication in a variety of contexts by performing these exercises regularly.

1. Conversational Dutch Dialogues: Over 100 Dutch Conversations and Short Stories – By Lingo Mastery

CHAPTER 6

Additional Resources to Aid in Learning and Improving Your Dutch

Learning and honing your Dutch can be facilitated by a plethora of tools that accommodate varying learning preferences and skill levels. Here's a comprehensive list of further resources:

Online Platforms and Apps:

1. **Duolingo:** A popular app offering gamified language lessons and exercises, suitable for beginners and intermediate learners.

2. **Babbel:** Provides structured Dutch courses with interactive exercises focusing on conversation skills and grammar.

3. **Rosetta Stone:** Known for immersive learning, it offers Dutch courses using a dynamic immersion method.

4. **Memrise:** Utilizes spaced repetition and mnemonic techniques to help memorize vocabulary and phrases.

Language Learning Websites:

1. **DutchPod101:** Offers audio and video lessons, podcasts, and resources for learners at various levels.

2. **LearnDutch.org:** Provides free lessons, grammar explanations, vocabulary exercises, and audio files for pronunciation practice.

3. **NT2 Exam Preparation:** Specifically designed for those preparing for the NT2 Dutch language proficiency exams.

Textbooks and Workbooks:

1. **"Complete Dutch" by Teach Yourself:** A comprehensive self-study course covering various aspects of Dutch grammar, vocabulary, and culture.

2. **"Colloquial Dutch" by Bruce Donaldson:** Focuses on everyday Dutch used in conversational

contexts, accompanied by audio resources.

3. **"Nederlands in Gang" Series:** A set of textbooks focusing on the Dutch language and culture, suitable for beginners.

Dutch Media and Cultural Content:

1. **Dutch TV Shows and Movies:** Watching Dutch series or films with subtitles can improve listening skills and familiarize learners with colloquial expressions.

2. **Dutch Radio and Podcasts:** Listening to Dutch radio stations or podcasts aids in understanding spoken Dutch and current affairs.

3. **Books and Newspapers in Dutch:** Reading Dutch literature, newspapers, or online articles helps expand vocabulary and comprehension skills.

Language Exchange and Conversation Practice:

1. **Tandem:** A language exchange app connecting learners worldwide with native Dutch speakers for language practice.

2. **HelloTalk:** Allows language exchange through text, voice messages, and video calls with native Dutch speakers.

Tutoring and Online Courses:

1. **Private Tutors:** Platforms like iTalki or Preply offer access to Dutch tutors for personalized lessons and guidance.

2. **University Courses and MOOCs:** Platforms like Coursera or edX often host Dutch language courses designed by universities, offering structured learning experiences.

Social Media and Online Communities:

1. **Reddit (r/learndutch):** A subreddit community for Dutch learners to ask questions, share resources, and practice the language.

2. **Language Forums and Facebook Groups:** Joining language forums or Facebook groups dedicated to learning Dutch facilitates interaction with fellow learners and native speakers.

Exploring these diverse materials and integrating them into your Dutch language learning process according to your preferences and learning style can greatly improve your language proficiency and comprehension of different cultures. A comprehensive Dutch language learning experience will result from the combination and regular use of these resources.

CHAPTER 7

Key Points Highlighting the Importance and Benefits of Learning Dutch

To sum up, choosing to study Dutch is a rewarding undertaking that leads to improved communication, cultural immersion, and personal development. Learning the Dutch language allows people to interact with other Dutch-speaking communities and access a lively culture. Below is a synopsis of the main ideas emphasizing the value and advantages of learning Dutch:

Practicality and Everyday Interactions:

- **Social Integration:** Speaking Dutch facilitates social interactions, enabling individuals to connect and build relationships within the Dutch-speaking community.

- **Navigating Daily Life:** Proficiency in Dutch is invaluable for accessing services, shopping, and handling administrative tasks in Dutch-speaking regions.

Cultural Integration and Understanding:

- **Appreciating Dutch Culture:** Learning Dutch provides insights into Dutch customs, traditions, and societal norms, fostering a deeper appreciation for Dutch culture.

- **Cultural Sensitivity:** Proficiency in the language promotes understanding and respect, which are crucial for integrating into the local culture.

Tips for Effective Learning:

- **Setting Realistic Goals:** Defining clear objectives aids in measuring progress and staying motivated.

- **Creating Study Routines:** Consistent practice through varied methods like speaking, listening, and immersion accelerates learning.

- **Utilizing Resources:** Leveraging diverse resources such as apps, language exchange, media, and tutoring enhances language proficiency.

Pronunciation and Language Mastery:

- Mastering Dutch sounds, intonation, and stress patterns contributes to effective communication and understanding in the language.

Learning Dutch is a fulfilling endeavor that not only promotes daily communication but also expands viewpoints, improves cross-cultural proficiency, and increases self-assurance in a variety of contexts. A rewarding and successful competency in speaking Dutch is achieved by embracing the language learning process with commitment, tolerance, and a readiness to fully immerse oneself in the language and culture.